far too big and far too wide.

sharing the love of Christ through a collection of
poetry and prose.

liliana faith whitley

ISBN: 9798394690891

manufactured in the united states of america.

cover design: liliana faith whitley

scripture excerpts from

The Holy Bible, New Living Translation. Tyndale House
Publishers © (original work published 1996).

to the givers,

may your passion for others never fade.

and to the one who never hesitated to point me back to
Jesus,

my very best friend,

kyle thomas holden.

preface.

the love of God has made a home in my heart and it is my deepest desire that it overflows into all of yours as well. we are all human and while our faith separates us from the world, there is strong reality and truth in the way we feel. and while our emotions do not define us or our character; they are and will always be valid.

i am here and this book is here to tell you that there is honesty in growth and healing and learning and failure. it takes courage to recognize these feelings and navigating them is all the more inspiring. may you always remember that nothing with God is too insurmountable.

there will be impossibility and sorrow and indescribable joy and heartbreak and tears and laughter and light and weakness and discovery and youth and wisdom. this life we have been so graciously given is irresistible, magnetic, and wild in beauty.

this life on earth is short and words are special and people are most precious. with words we are able to convey the very message of our hearts and i hope these pages bring you comfort and truth. these are the chapters of my life and i pray they fill your cup and that you may feel slightly less alone. praise be to Jesus for He willed it so. endless thank you to readers near and far.

you are life giving.

far too big and far too wide.

contents.

for so long

i failed to consider writing to be art.

for words lack color and depth and song

but over time i've come to know it to be

the most captivating.

because within these pages is my heart,

colorful and deep and like lyrics.

it's with poetry i gained the ability to sing

to the melody of my heart strings.

so the contents of this book

is everything i was, everything i am and hope to be.

tyj.

far too big and far too wide.

part one:

our suffering.

much of this chapter rests in the reality of feeling
worldly emotion that deeply impacts our hearts. it's
hurtful, it's raw, it's real, it's honest. much of my walk
with Christ has lead me to feel guilty about feeling
anything other than joy but i have graciously come to
know and i am here to tell you that there is truth inside
of you. to feel guilty or shameful or sorry for feeling
the way you do is to miss the point of the gospel. from
everlasting to everlasting, our Father in heaven will
hold your hand in the midst of your suffering. you are
not alone. and you don't have to feel everything that
you feel alone. this is the heartbreak and the loneliness
and the doubting. this is the very real understanding
that feeling is fleeting but joy that comes from the Lord
is eternal.

there is power in the name of Jesus

and it is evident in your weakness.

oh how His steadfast mercy becomes the most
prominent in your weakness!

His passion for you lead Him atop the hill,

praise pouring from His mouth.

His passion of you lead Him upon a cross,

love pouring down His hands.

His passion for you is real

and this power is profoundly yours.

some days in may be your brokenness that keeps your feet at the cross and that is okay.

you are not called to perfection,

or emotionless,

or grey,

or unwavering.

let His grace be sufficient enough.

you were unmoved by me.

when i showed you what i was hesitant to bring to the light once more,

unlike people before,

you didn't leave.

you didn't walk away.

you didn't run the other direction.

you didn't want out.

you adopted the compassion of Christ and

you stayed.

and for the very first time,

i saw and felt love.

in its truest form.

complex and honest and raw,

but simple because

you stayed.

far too big and far too wide.

my place in your life

has been made abundantly clear.

and i have accepted that

when it's convenient for you,

i will be here.

while i have let you go,

you have not lost me.

i might be your last choice in your life

and that's fine,

but know that you are still welcome in mine.

on the days when it feels impossible to show up,

because there will be days,

show up for your future self.

let them look back and draw inspiration from this page in your story.

and on days when even that is just too much,

i pray that you show up here,

before the cross.

show up for your Father.

let Him guide you along the precious path that He has so effortlessly created for you,

show up for Him.

far too big and far too wide.

heart of glass.

God willing,

i found what you so carelessly dropped

and healed it completely.

what you left for all color to fade,

i painted back in vivid, striking streaks of accomplished recovery.

like a puzzle, i've placed each piece back together.

in the time that you had him,

you tried to love him.

but i am glad that it was me who picked up the fragments of his broken heart.

i've cleaned up your mess.

i've repaired the trust that you severed.

she's good.

she's happy.

she's sweet.

she's kind.

oh, to have an unchanging, steadfast soul

still sweet despite the influence.

it's like modern day treasure

to find someone true.

someone who holds open the doors

even for those who have slammed it in her face.

someone who weeps for another's loss.

because it *is* possible

to love with a pretty heart

and to remain kind

when what you receive in return is anything but

less than good.

less that happy.

less than sweet.

and less than kind.

feeling broken does not make you a broken person.
feeling forgotten does not make you a forgotten
person.
feeling lonely does not make you alone.

you may have felt all of these things but you are also
incredibly resilient.
you are strong and brave. you can do hard things. you
are thoughtful and kind.
and i hope you learn to not let anyone make you feel
otherwise.
but know that you are none of these things without
Jesus.

He is a perfect Father.
our God is gentle. He gives grace beyond measure. He
loves the lost and brings them to the light.
He sits with us while we cry on the floor. He sees you
falling apart and mends you in all of your brokenness.
He is patient and forgiving and when no one else
understands,

Jesus Christ understands.

the water was numbingly cold.

you were welcomingly warm.

we both jumped.

an old soul

you said.

you left me like the water that day.

you took your kind affection and didn't look back.

now i am

icy

bitter

sharp

and i feel like i'm drowning on dry land.

and when you feel that all you have left to share is the possession of a name

and the reminiscence of memories,

may you learn to gracefully say goodbye.

may you learn to love them from a distance.

life is too short to continue to share in intimacy with those you have outgrown.

the heart i wear on my sleeve no longer belongs to you.

i don't look for you in the crowds.

you are not the brightest star in my sky of friendship.

and i thought i would be sad

when i finally had the strength to choose myself

but i think some time ago

i learned to listen for footsteps.

and the sound of my feet as i walk away prove all of my
doubts about you.

far too big and far too wide.

and in that moment,

just before the sun reaches the horizon,

i saw the beautiful possibility

of us.

but like all imaginary scenarios,

the sun set.

any chance left to fade.

the light was swallowed into the darkness of night,

into nothingness,

surrounded only by the glimmer of the stars

serving as reminders

of what could have been.

and then i realized,

i am simply married to the perception of you,

the version of you i convinced myself

that you were.

that i forced myself to believe.

that i created in my head.

far too big and far too wide.

after all,

it's perfectly refined.

but with everyone's everything

easily accessible at our fingertips,

how could you not,

it's only a couple clicks,

to inspect side by side,

your life and mine.

in the midst of being strong for everyone else,

sometimes i forget that it's okay

to let my eyes water.

to let my shoulders cave in.

to let my head bow.

it's okay to let yourself be human.

to let yourself feel.

and break.

and heal.

but learn to be strong for yourself too.

far too big and far too wide.

how is it she's made of honey and salt?
both sweet and aflame?

you can be fierce and assertive
and still allow the grace of God to flow from your
heart.

you can walk away from draining people and still wish
them an abundance of love.

you can put on the amour of God to conquer your
battles.

i often think of the man you wish you had the chance of knowing just a little bit longer.

the one i wish could have watched you grow into the incredibly gracious man you are today.

i am sometimes saddened by the truth that i will never meet him.

i wonder what he was like and although your barley knew him,

i feel strongly that you are more similar than you realize.

i hope i am the one he dreamt you would find.

far too big and far too wide.

there are people who are too busy for you.
there are people who are too unconcerned with you.
there are people who become distant when more effort
may be required.
there are people who do not have the maturity to sit
down and talk with you.

but there will also be people who hold your hand and
pray to the One most high.
there will be people who walk with you in the rain.
there will be people who speak truth and wisdom over
you.
there will be people who, in everything that they do,
point you to Jesus.

keep them close, hold them near.
seek community with people who seek community with
you.

there is more to you than yesterday.

there will be days when you don't feel joy or peace.
there will be many moments when you don't feel all of
the things that God promises us.
but He will sustain you until the next day.
He will give you enough grace until the next day.
from dusk to dawn, He will carry you.
and like the dew upon the leaves,
His mercies are new each morning.

there is more to you than yesterday.

far too big and far too wide.

as you watched me struggle,

i watched you lose interest in me.

i watched you talk to me less.

i watched you walk out of my life.

i watched you leave.

and i let you.

my sin the nails

and my disobedience deep red.

oh Jesus!

hear my cry!

how can my soul express the gratitude?

my ransom a crown of thorns

and my debt forever paid,

hanging honorably upon the cross.

far too big and far too wide.

right now you cannot see the end of the road
but that doesn't mean it's not there.

right now it's dark
but that doesn't mean the sun will not rise again.

right now it won't stop raining
but that doesn't mean that it won't calm.

and if for a long time it *is* dark
and you feel stranded
and the rain never seems to slow,

know that you were made to praise Him in the storm.

remember where your help comes from.

happy birthday.

i adored everything about being a child.

and i recognized at the young age of ten that double digits wasn't all it was made out to be.

when others were excited, i was met with sorrow.

for i didn't want to leave behind everything i knew.

where smiles formed on the faces of others,

tears fell upon my own.

fearing change? maybe.

but it was the impending pressure of getting older that i was at odds with.

and so melancholy flowed

similar to the way the hint taste of salt reaches my mouth each july.

because while another year older means more freedom and new experiences,

to me,

it's leaving my upbringing

and parting from my childhood.

and i just cannot simply comprehend the celebration.

you're not a little girl anymore

at that,

my heart shatters.

far too big and far too wide.

slow.

like the way a storm rolls in.

first, it's gloomy and grey.

missing the presence of sunlight after all.

then the thunder sounds; bold,

signifying anger and betrayal.

shortly after,

the water works begin

and rain settles within the cracks of the pavement.

leaving traces of the past

lingering even by the scent of the air.

that's how you left me.

if you even actually left at all.

to not let the words of others change your heart

feels like achieving the impossible.

the way of the world

and the vast capacity for hurt,

all have the willing ability

to break your heart

in two.

so the scratches and the dents

inflicted by others

upon the goodness in you.

cannot count.

because if you let it contribute,

bitterness would put your kindness on mute.

maybe it was peer pressure or the longing need to fit in.

but i could see it within your actions.

the way you hesitated to give up everything good.

you have a desire to hold on to what once was.

that was beat by your choices,

and yet when away from the crowd,

when it's you and only you,

the desire remains.

your heart remains.

good and kind.

sweet and selfless.

grief is difficult.

it's confusing and somehow at the same time,

it seems to make sense.

you see,

grief can only be found where love once lived.

and i think that's beautiful.

i think that holding to this truth allows our broken heart to embrace grief -

in all of its aching.

and i think we can hold on to it for as long as we need to.

far too big and far too wide.

the words escaped his mouth softly

and with the same gentleness as the character of his heart;

it's real tears and valued emotions.

that was the first time she felt completely seen.

the first time she believed in trust.

the first time she was wholeheartedly loved.

she stood up from her puddle of overwhelming emotion and willingly walked into forever and more.

knowing that for all of her days to come,

the next time she found herself sitting on the floor,

it would be *his* hand that would help her to stand again.

she was golden

and he was the sun.

moving in harmony,

cut from the same star.

and still she protected her heart,

cautious.

-    it's always too good to be true.

far too big and far too wide.

unapologetic strength looks a lot like
letting yourself feel everything.
sometimes all at once
and sometimes for days at a time.

dear lost friend,

i once thought you'd stand by my side on one of the
most special days of my life. i would hand off my
bouquet and look down the line to the left and we
would exchange a glance that summed up all of our
love in one single moment.

but today, in one single moment, i glanced at you and
that love wasn't there. you were once close and now
you are far. i'll still love you like you're close but you
aren't invited to the next chapter of my life.

i think that to be there for my most special day, you
should have been there for my worst.

sincerely,

a girl who knows who she is now and what she
deserves.

faultless and hollow.

you tell me i am one but i feel like the latter.

what do i have left to give?

my heart is empty and you don't want it.

if emotions controlled the weather,

i am spiraling.

i am a tornado of seemingly inescapable feeling.

it's pouring now, i'm crying out to you.

i pace and the wind picks up.

screaming on the inside,

i can't contain it,

i let it out.

across the sky above,

thunder cracks and so does my heart.

hiding behind the lightning,

there you stand.

confidently pursuing me in the middle of my storm.

there is this fear.

of letting people down.
letting them drown.
dragging them down to drown with you.

of what they think.
what they perceive.
what are they going to believe?

of failure.
of going all in and falling for everyone to see.
to watch you like they've been waiting.

of never quite being enough.
good enough,
smart, pretty, friendly, kind enough.
she's just kind of.

you *are* going to drown and fall short and fail
but giving up isn't an option.
letting yourself down isn't an option.
standing in your own way isn't an option.

believing in fear isn't an option.

far too big and far too wide.

to be sorry to know each other's pain

is to be glad to know each other's healing.

you get to choose.

you get to choose who you let into your life.

you get to choose how someone's actions make you feel.

you get to choose who you allow into your heart.

you get to choose how much you share.

you get to choose to stand up for yourself.

you get to choose who deserves to know you fully.

you get to choose when to walk away.

you get to choose boundaries.

you get to choose who you follow.

you get to choose how you treat people who break your heart.

you get to choose yourself.

far too big and far too wide.

we were never meant to have it all

but we were meant to have Him.

the God of *all* grace will not forsake you.

and when it all seems to fall apart;

His grace is immeasurably more.

His love is immeasurably more.

He is merciful and sweet and kind and Lord of all

and He will never give up on you.

do not let anyone undermine your empathy.

preserve your heart,

sensitivity is special.

don't you dare change it for the world.

far too big and far too wide.

i'm stranded alone in this place

but as my body is searching for its breath,

i am reminded to consider the lilies.

because like the rise and fall of my chest,

i begin to notice

the rise and fall of the sun.

and the rise and fall of the tide.

and the rise of the flowers during spring and fall of the
flowers during autumn.

there is a rise and fall of the rain

and there is a rise and fall of the moon.

so know that you are supposed rise and fall too.

you were not made to stand tall forever,

not even the lilies were made to do so.

so when your emotions rise and fall,

no matter the frequency,

know that its natural.

you're supposed to rise and fall.

i would be lying if i said i didn't look forward to seeing
you for those two weeks once a year.

you are always so effortlessly nice,

right and just and good.

just the same as when we left.

you make sure to never leave without a wave goodbye

and i think, maybe, that somehow makes it all hurt just
a little bit more.

you told me not to waste all my imagination on you

but when i see you where i met you,

how could i not?

think about where it could have gone.

you and me.

it made sense,

right and just and good.

far too big and far too wide.

even when you're going through devastating trial

and you cry out for help,

and they still choose to walk away.

i pray you choose amiability.

i pray you choose kindness.

i pray you choose forgiveness.

i used your words like sutures to mend all of the parts
of me that i neglected

and when you stopped speaking,

i was left to bleed out.

my open wounds lacked stitching.

fast forward and i've learned that your band-aid of
words came too late before.

lacerations begging for praise and affirmation.

how did i not recognize you were only causing more
pain?

far too big and far too wide.

know that the pain you're feeling right now,

Jesus has hurt this way once too.

not only can He *see* what you're going through,

but He *understands* exactly what it's like to be

betrayed

forgotten

helpless

unfriended

disliked

let down

deceived

work of art.

what a devastating luxury;

to feel.

people will tell you it's too much and you'll find
yourself wanting to internalize any emotion deemed too
dramatic or too real.

instead i urge you to put them on display for everyone
to see.

you're an unperfect picture painted from a pallet of
praises.

those who possess the ability to appreciate

will gaze upon you like art in a museum.

but unlike a canvas on a wall,

human nature and feeling

is not auctioned or perfectly framed or permanent.

it's ever-changing and fierce and honest and never the
same and completely yours.

far too big and far too wide.

so sit in the pouring rain and let Him pick you up.

sit in the pouring rain and let Him dance with you.

sit in the pouring rain and let Him tell you that

it will pass, the sun will shine again, this is only but a
season

and He is here with you through it all.

and even if they choose not to celebrate your wins,
no matter the size,
i hope you'll clap for them anyway.
i hope you'll appreciate their success anyway.
i hope you'll smile at them anyway.
i hope you'll congratulate them anyway.

and i hope you choose to love them anyway.

the story was perfectly predictable.

i often tend to imagine what it would have been like

to fall in love with you.

looking for you in the crowd

because alone, the silence would sound far too loud.

although than i had wished we were on the same team,

i know now that my future holds more than your

paper dreams.

just because your innocence has been stolen
does not mean that you have been left to swim
upstream.

just because someone made you feel unworthy
does not mean that reigns true in the Kingdom.

just because your tears fell by the words of another
does not mean your strength has disappeared.

He calms the waters.
He knows your worth.
He gives you undeniable strength.

far too big and far too wide.

i am overwhelmed by the nearness of you.

but it's not the you i once sought.

no.

for that version of you doesn't exist anymore.

not in the way he should.

its nostalgic almost,

you look like you but you're completely different.

so now i am left seeking you

in pursuit of imagined good.

i know now you'll never measure

but how can i not picture it?

when i used to hear your name

i knew with good it was tied all the same.

looking back at it all,

i would rather feel everything than nothing at all.

the hurt and the love.

the pain and the joy.

because a breaking heart still carries a beat.

and no matter how quiet or well-hidden it may seem,

it's a melody that deserves to be heard.

it's only mildly intoxicating.

the way our fate is written in careful letters.

and your touch is but a whisper dancing across my
skin,

lasting long even after your hands abandon my own.

simple and brief.

tangible

but utterly unattainable.

the Spirit is alive and well.

for it lives in my very veins,

falls from my tears.

and for all of my days,

is the breath in my lungs.

far too big and far too wide.

i was captivated by you because your words were
written with skill,

no spoken by truth.

manipulation came natural to you.

it wasn't violence or force that gave you power

but the repetitive false declarations.

it was your illusions

that filled the gaps of my ignorance.

in the house in-between,

she learned the complicated,
difficult,
heart wrenching,
heavy,
and confusing act of trusting.
trusting the Lord in her deepest distress taught her to
praise Him within the aching.

in the house in-between,

her knees hit the ground more than ever before.
only when we have shared in His suffering will we
share within His glory.

far too big and far too wide.

he was abundant in love

and she was scarce.

where he was infinite,

she was limited.

with a heavy heart,

he can accept

that everything she couldn't give him

was all he ever wanted.

your very burden is what qualifies you to come to Jesus.

He is the most

tender.

open.

welcoming.

accommodating.

understanding.

accepting.

willing.

gentle.

He astounds and sustains us over and over and over again.

far too big and far too wide.

you might recognize the lack of good in the midst of it
all

but i urge you to know that it is

promised

that Jesus will come again.

all the while,

may we choose to praise the Savior.

we know His judgment is

holy and divine and perfect.

> even when we do not understand.

part two:

our stillness.

this is the middle. the in-between. what i have a feeling most our days look like. after we've encountered the love of Christ but not quite grasped the glory of all of His promises. the part of our life we can feel ourselves growing and learning what it means to walk in holy obedience. this is the friends and the family. this is the mosaic that makes up everything we are. the influence of the people we love most. this is the falling in love and the day dreams. this is the seeking more. more relationships. more honesty. more time with our Father.

let us lead a humble life.

let us take the hands of others

and run to the heavens

into our Fathers' arms.

far too big and far too wide.

i hope that

like the salt in the sea,

You take up all of me.

i hope that

for every grain of sand on the shore,

i will proclaim Your name.

and i hope that

when the tide covers the beaches and reveals the sand
again,

i'll be reminded of Your steadfast, unchanging,
constant, and all-consuming love.

your mind will always believe anything you tell it.

give it grace,

give it faith,

give it truth.

far too big and far too wide.

because the good always outweighs the bad

and even through all the cards you were dealt,

it was you that still somehow made my heart melt.

third.

address the letter to you.

back when we sang in middle school

to taylor swifts' wildest dreams

before anyone influenced our self-esteem.

long summers on the lake

turned to mutual heart ache.

unforgivable words and when i became third.

yet even looking back,

discarding what could have been,

to put a price on the love

and to measure the laughter

would be to put it in a box.

and so even though it's without me,

your future is bright

and although i watch from afar,

i know that we're alright.

far too big and far too wide.

may we always continue to love and give and
encourage.

to vow to never change,

to continue to build our life upon the foundation of
love and clap for others.

we cannot alter the way we love simply because others
do not have the capacity within their heart

to give the way we do.

to listen the way we do.

to love the way we do.

today i want to remind you that you are right where you are supposed to be.

you are right in the middle of what you prayed for.

you are right where our God wants you.

far too big and far too wide.

i always have so much i want to say,

so much i want to tell you.

in the minutes leading up to seeing you,

i'll plan it all out,

imagining the way you'll respond.

but when you're in front of me,

i seem to forget how to speak.

i don't know how to be around you like i'm not in love with you.

you make my face warm.

you make my speech stutter.

you make me forget i even wanted to say anything at all.

not everything is meant to be long lasting.

not everything is meant to be beautiful forever.

people will walk in your life and

some will stay until the very end.

and some only for a little while.

despite this,

we will keep going,

we will keep giving grace,

and we will keep loving.

far too big and far too wide.

you'll realize the present will feel nostalgic

when everything around you seems to move in slow
motion

and the sounds of song and conversation fade into the
distance.

like somehow this moment has already been date
stamped

and filed away in memory for safe keeping.

a little too aware of the ticking clock,

you'll soak up every second

and attempt to stay in this little pocket of time

before it lies permanently in the past.

today i crave patience.

i want to rest within this moment.

i wish to be content where i am,

to lean into the perfect timing.

may i learn to love the waiting

and to trust the Lord our God.

far too big and far too wide.

my heart has been rearranged.

or maybe it's always been like this

but either way,

you brought out the best in me.

you made room for me in the world

and you told me that it's okay to take up space.

you taught me to fight for the good

and to never take anything too seriously.

you showed me to care less about what other people
think and to care more about what the Father thinks.

it's endearing to be loved by you.

on the plane

headed miles away,

i was so wildly unsure

about you,

about us.

but eighty-four days later,

i had roses in my hand

and i was absolutely certain

about you,

about us.

far too big and far too wide.

and if your faith makes you look foolish,

so be it.

when it begins to rain,

they will ask you where your joy comes from.

what a privilege to show them.

this is what you were made for.

her face lit up with warmth

like the sky surrounding the sun setting before her.

she never tired of observing the beauty of the passing day.

her repeating reaction each evening

sparked my sense for simplicity.

the colors that washed over the city

enkindled her longing for nature.

watching her in awe.

and now, each time i see the pink rays above,

i too light up and rejoice in the promise of goodness.

far too big and far too wide.

so God, would you teach me?

teach me to wholeheartedly surrender and be fully
devoted to You.

how is it you love me more on my worst day than when we first met?

how is it you care for my broken heart just the same as when i smile?

how is it you'd prefer a devastating trial with me than happiness without me?

how is it you've become so willing to go to war for my love?

far too big and far too wide.

early mornings when the house was full

meant the news was playing

and on the couch was my favorite person

and i, his.

good morning pumpkin.

wrinkled hands showcasing his life's accomplishments

held a mug of cheap coffee.

tradition called for a taste by the dip of his finger,

recollection tells me it was warm and strong

similar to the relationship not many get the pleasure to
experience.

gratitude forever remains in my heart.

i fell into happiness in this town.

i once thought that i would have to chase and track down everything i ever desired.

that i would have to catch and claim it before it was out of reach.

but right here,

with you,

is where i seemed to just walk right into what i needed.

like it was here all along waiting for me to recognize it.

i think that's how i know it's meant for me and only me.

no more running,

just simply receiving what the Lord our God has laid before me.

far too big and far too wide.

everything she is

embodies the definition of grace.

with blue eyes and blonde hair,

she is a societal beauty.

but in conjunction with her ability to appreciate

even those who have caused her pain,

the only one i've ever known with a heart

willing to give beyond.

heaven sent,

i would say,

that we crossed paths.

when you're driving through the rain,

water is forcibly falling all around you.

passing under a highway, there is a moment.

a brief second where the sounds of the storm pause

and everything is still, quiet, and safe.

it's calming.

and then you're walking across the beach,

waves are crashing all around you.

taking a step back to notice and appreciate that

no matter the circumstance,

the waves never seem to stop kissing the shore.

always coming back,

gracing the sand with the touch of salt

and everything is still, quiet, and safe.

it's calming.

your presence is like that.

your love is like that.

far too big and far too wide.

the trees lose their leaves and still they color green.

the sea loses its wave and still the tide rises.

the sky can cry and still paint the horizon.

but your capacity for forgiveness is beyond the trees
and the sea and the sky.

you forgive like it's your second nature.

you forgive like you've got pools of grace spilling over.

you forgive like it's your duty to protect the people
who purposefully scratched your heart.

and i think you learned that from the only man to ever
walk this earth whose soul was perfectly pure.

from the One who created the trees and the sea and the
sky.

her drive and dedication seemed to strike everyone around her.

she knew what she wanted and worked hard to achieve it.

ambitious was her soul,

set in her ways

and true to herself.

she was her future

and they were inspired.

far too big and far too wide.

her embrace was genuine and warm,
a gentle reminder that you belonged.

she was capable of tough love,
a strong reminder of your potential.

it's different now that she's joined the stars.

her love shows up in different forms now.

i'll forever miss our walks and talks

but i hear her in music and feel her in movement.

i see her in smiles and in glittering blue.

hope.

i am living for it.

i am holding onto it.

i can see it so clearly.

even on this side of heaven.

far too big and far too wide.

he thrived off of consistency

and she admired how the rise of the sun was always
followed by its setting.

they had a fate to fall together.

i can see it so plainly.

your black suit made complete by the smile upon your
face.

i'm wearing white.

surrounded by all of our favorite people

under the painted sky,

confetti on the floor and lilies form that little flower
store.

it's perfect,

everything i dreamed it would be,

for the glory of the kingdom.

and it feels like slow motion.

you and me.

toasting to forever.

i've always been discouraged

at how quickly the sky's canvas of color fades.

after all, sunsets aren't made to last through the night.

and so i've taken notice to appreciate them just a little
more.

although what's above has a tendency

to change within seconds,

it's a gentle reminder that i too, am constantly

transforming,

growing,

and learning.

she gives beyond her limits.

she shows true grace and empathy.

to be the constant light surrounded by the darkness of others

takes incomparable strength.

she is a hero for she has a gift unlike any other,

capable of loving even those

that cannot love you back.

she is my mother.

far too big and far too wide.

i can see His heart in everything you do

and for that i am helplessly drawn to you.

let this be a reminder that it is not too late.

your path is long.

and it does not have to measure and match those around you.

your goals are still achievable.

He has planned so much for you.

far too big and far too wide.

somehow over the years,

you both have become brave and adventurous.

maybe you've always been that way but

i admire that spirit of yours.

you're not afraid to fail and the future excites you.

i am forever grateful we are friends above all.

you both tower over me and excel in many areas i do not.

i look up, literally,

in awe.

aware that you are a steady support and i know that even within your adventure filled future,

that will remain constant.

there are realists and there are optimists.

pragmatists and idealists.

and then there are the poets.

the souls of the world who live for possibility,

the dreamers of the good,

of what can be.

nonconformity or wishful thinking?

maybe.

but romantic if nothing else.

beautiful and charming.

passionate

if nothing else.

far too big and far too wide.

the break in the clouds.

that's where i get to see you.

i know you're looking down,

stopping by,

taking a peak,

just saying hi.

things have been good here,

better now that you're near.

you are like my gold crayon.

the one i use to color the stars

and the sparks of the fire.

the sun rays and the glisten in your eyes.

the one i save for last and never want to run out of.

far too big and far too wide.

day 62 of 84.

missing you has become my cup of coffee in the
mornings.
missing you has become my day dream.
missing you has become my night time comfort.

until i see you again.
i imagine your embrace.
i imagine us together.
i imagine our life,

the one that will last forever.

when the very surface below our feet begin to cave in

and the stars above fall,

even in the midst of it all,

i know you will try to find me,

just as i am looking for you.

i am left seeking a house with a crowded table.

and enough love to go around.

and enough joy to keep people laughing.

and enough holiness to make them want to come back.

i am left seeking a place where hurt is welcome and hearts are healed.

looking back, it's difficult to fathom.

the bravery it took to look at their life and realize they deserved more.

to decide to make a change

for the sake of three children

and the future of their family.

for this place granted them more

than what they came for.

and for that i will always hold the highest respect.

far too big and far too wide.

he will spend his life falling in love with her.

over and over and over again

and deeper again.

God has granted you the choice to move through your days striving for freedom and joy.

do not let what the world or your past self may tell you

prevent you from experiencing the freedoms and the joys.

make use of your time here.

far too big and far too wide.

you are my good,

he said,

to be plentiful in love and to give it all to you

is all i've ever wanted to do.

you are my good.

even from one thousand five hundred and thirty-nine miles away,

i saw your smile and i heard your laughter.

some days it's what kept me going amidst the chaos of summer.

i know we aren't who we were last may,

but i think they'd be proud of us.

you once asked me what i wanted.
just the two of us sitting under the stars,
i was still nervous.
i didn't know what i really wanted then.
i don't think i had ever thought about it,
no one had ever asked me.

the school was dimly lit and we watched as people
slowly turned their bedroom lights off.
the darkness has called for the end of the day,
but we still sat and talked and yearned to be closer.

i know what i want now
and it's simple really.
just you
and me
for as long as we live.

i'll be twenty once and never again.

so take my hand

and twirl me around in the rain.

let's be hopeless in love.

kiss me gently,

once,

twice,

one hundred times.

far too big and far too wide.

he was comparable to a sunflower.

like somehow the light always hit his face at the right time.

the kind of bright that makes you want to look twice,

makes you want to be better.

he shared a little piece of his heart each time he smiled.

his words were sugar;

sweet, kind, and always honest.

because he believes everyone's light deserves to be seen.

his eyes were sunshine that did not hesitate to place patience upon those who were dim.

he was like the color yellow.

to look at the world with an ordinary lens

is to miss the magic of the mediocre.

far too big and far too wide.

how can you watch the sunrise and not see endless possibility?

it is my wish for you to see the stars as physical proof of accomplished dreams.

to hear laughter and allow it to be the melody of your life.

to feel the overwhelming sense of satisfaction when another smiles.

be sentimental.

be intentional.

be tenderhearted and affectionate and romantic.

part three:

our salvation.

what is waiting for you is so bright. and much of this
chapter emphasizes that. the light at the end of the
tunnel. the goodness of God. if i could go back in time
and give myself pages of encouragement when i
doubted my ability or self-worth or as i walked through
hard seasons, i would give her this chapter. this is the
healing. the rejoicing and the recognition of our Lord
and Savior, Jesus Christ. this is the homecoming.

i am living in constant pursuit of my Creator

and i am completely undone.

by His majesty.

by His willingness to love broken hearts back to life.

by His endless effort to know me.

by His handy works of art before my very eyes.

i am living in the reality of Jesus Christ

and i am completely undone.

far too big and far too wide.

a common misconception is that the Kingdom in
heaven awaits for those who have acquired enough
good deeds like points on a score board

or maybe for the ones that said all of the right things
and followed all of the rules.

no my dear, there is a spot saved specifically for *you*.

nobody is keeping score.

you will never be too far gone.

you will never be too broken.

you will *never* be too far away from the welcoming arms
of Jesus Christ.

each day we are given a brand-new opportunity

to bring a smile to someone's face

and hearing that laughter might just be the greatest joy
in all of humanity.

far too big and far too wide.

the world has and will continue to tell you that

you are unworthy.

in all of the ways you wish to be seen,

the world will dim the lights.

yes, it is true that you are of no value alone

but with Jesus Christ, you are of endless worth.

oh, with Jesus you are free.

with Him you are seen.

for He shines the light on you.

look at My daughter, My beautiful soul.

we are sons and daughters of the King most high
crowned with steadfast love and mercy.

benevolently redeemed.

far too big and far too wide.

let the One who created you

be the One who defines you.

nothing on this earth is worth believing otherwise.

may we sit before the cross and believe within our
hearts

the incomprehensible love

of the life

it once held.

may we carry that sacrifice through all of our days,

knowing our life is the result.

may we forever be the hands and the feet.

the body of Christ.

far too big and far too wide.

know that when you find yourself in the valley,

you are more than gifted.

for God does not call the equipped but rather,

He equips the called.

you have what it takes and there is not a single trial too
difficult when Jesus is standing by your side.

she doesn't spread joy just to *appear* joyful.

she spreads joy like wildfire because she *is* joy and everything she touches sparks the flame.

she will set the world ablaze and leave it a little brighter than it was before.

far too big and far too wide.

you have a mind and soul capable of grace beyond
measure.

you are so much more than you think you are.

take heart in knowing that where your very feet are
standing right now,

God has been there before.

He has,

and will forever,

go before you.

this life will bring unrequited love and devastating loss,

but there will also be unexpected hope and endless fulfillment in the name of Jesus.

i am a child of the King of kings.

and so are you.

i have a seat at His table.

and so do you.

i am swimming is freedom and i owe it all to our Father in heaven.

libertas.

it feels light.

like floating but not quite flying.

no, my feet are planted.

a firm foundation.

touching the rich soil as i tend to my garden of morals.

my chains have broken into a blossom of deliverance.

i have been set free by the grace of God.

far too big and far too wide.

it's simple, it runs deep, and it is enough.

    -    the gospel

in this space between heaven and hell,

we have the ability to change the hearts of countless individuals and show them the love of Christ.

let us be patient.

let us be merciful.

let us be kind.

let us be compassionate.

let us be gentle.

and despite it all,

let us be forgiving.

far too big and far too wide.

perhaps at this moment in time

He is reminding you

to look up,

to seek things above

and to fix your eyes upon his promises.

so celebrate with strangers,

sit with the rejected,

walk each other home,

and carry their burdens.

far too big and far too wide.

i want to spend every waking moment beside You.

let my every breathe and all of my minutes

radiate Your love.

you are capable of a life in the sunshine.

you are capable of living in simplicity.

enjoy where God has placed you and the life before you will always be fulfilling.

you are capable.

far too big and far too wide.

her attitude painted the world golden.

the aura of everything she's made of

lingers even in the darkest of places.

for she was the gift of life.

i didn't realize how fast i had been running

until i was met with exhaustion.

i didn't realize how much i didn't hesitate to play the game.

not just to keep up but

trying to win,

to be first,

to be the best.

my footsteps have slowed now

and my heartbeat is steady.

i am no longer anxious for a life not meant for me.

i have won on my own terms.

i have won my own race.

i am walking in newness of life.

with a brand-new heart.

far too big and far too wide.

healed from His wounds

and saved by His grace,

in the midst of it all,

may we always *choose* to love.

though i am not where i thought i'd be,

i still believe this life is everything beautiful

and i will continue to declare that You are everything
good.

far too big and far too wide.

Your word remains the same

now and forever.

not once did i imagine my love to be enough to go to
war for,

but You fought for me.

without hesitation,

without expectation,

You fought for me.

and You have proved me wrong time and time again.

You showed me what it looks like to never give up on
what matters most.

You showed me what it looks like to love
unconditionally.

how undeserving am i to have been thought worthy
enough to die for?

far too big and far too wide.

getting the chance to come across another individual

and hearing their stories

and being present with them in the moment,

that is *the most* precious gift from above.

sitting in Your presence

makes me wonder

why didn't i sit down sooner.

why i didn't choose You sooner.

why i didn't tell people about You sooner.

and every time, i am left feeling like our time together is fulfilling and good and *necessary*.

i pour out my gratitude.

my words on paper.

there is prayer spilling from my pencil

and mercy from my mouth.

far too big and far too wide.

is there anything better or more precious than loving people?

because being kind and loving one another

is the easiest,

most beautiful thing we get to do.

it is when we start believing

that our purpose and happiness

are equated with achievement and good works

that we tend to forget

it is paid.

no, for our purpose and happiness

are found within the One who laid His life

to grant us ours.

far too big and far too wide.

i followed my heart before

and it never quite seemed to lead me to

places or people that offered what my soul desired
most.

and when nowhere felt like home,

i didn't know where i was supposed to go.

                                  i ran to the Father

                          and He taught me that

eternity is our home.

i may not be beautiful to the world

but i am beautiful to You.

what does the world matter if it is You

that will forever be the compass of my life?

what does the world matter if it is You

that had the creative hand willing enough for me?

far too big and far too wide.

i pray we never get lost in the applause,

let your victory result in praise.

may we always owe it all to the One who willed it to be
so.

He knows it all beginning to end.

become the woman,

become the man

that God has made you to be.

become the person God has written upon your heart.

far too big and far too wide.

with everything i am,

i want to give You my heart,

i am proud of you.

what an act to faith it is for you to move forward.

even if today it may be all that you do,

what an act of faith it is to put one foot in front of the other.

to continue

to progress

to make way

to prove yourself

only to yourself.

despite it all, what an act of faith.

you. are. brave.

far too big and far too wide.

may your judgment be scarce to find fault in beauty.

our God delights in the details of your life.

by the Lord above,

here and now,

you are seen.

far too big and far too wide.

He spoke and it was so.

while our sins are many,

His mercy is so much more.

the Son of suffering wept.

the Son of suffering held His head high.

the Son of suffering healed.

the Son of suffering forgave.

the Son of suffering rejoiced.

far too big and far too wide.

to the people in my corner;

God was more than generous when He gave me you.

i rejoice in knowing you will remain proud even if i
accomplish nothing.

for an extended period of time,

i sat in my hurt.

i looked to my circumstances for my joy.

my circumstances were not joyful.

today,

i abandoned my hurt at the door.

all i had to do was knock

and Jesus was waiting – no,

inviting

me to the other side.

i look to Him for my joy.

He *is* joyful.

far too big and far too wide.

God deliberately chooses the wounded.

He chooses the one in the most unlikely of places.

He chooses the imperfect

and prepares them for a glorious life.

and even if it remains unrequited,

i will always thank the Lord for giving me the chance to love you.

far too big and far too wide.

there comes a time,

when all of the people and all of the places,

the mornings and the evenings,

all of the heartbreak and all of the glory,

and all of the hours in-between,

amount to some sort of elimination of any fear for the future.

you have experienced the goodness of God.

let that be a testament to where you are headed.

you have walked through trial just the same as you climbed to your highest of moments.

you have learned to trust your Father in heaven.

for He is good and will be with you through it all.

it is one of the greatest privileges of my life,

getting to know You.

far too big and far too wide.

deliverance.

resting on my heart, it feels like a new beginning.
i am moving forward.
i can see the light at the end of the tunnel and i am
making small strides to reach it.

i am not done.
the Lord is not done with me!

i am leaving it in the past.
i will glance back but i will not stay there.
what is behind me has molded me
like a potter molds clay.

i thank Jesus for carrying me through these months

with the same strength and serenity

as when He bore our cross and carried our shame.

how can i dwell upon my suffering when the name
above all names

has felt nails through His bones

and when the weight of the world was placed atop His
head

and pierced through His skin?

far too big and far too wide.

because with Me

you are so endlessly enough.

- His love

He never fails.

He never leaves.

He never gives up.

He's never late.

He never disappoints.

He never turns His back on you.

far too big and far too wide.

when the skies turned orange

and the stars began to peak through,

i know it to be on fire for You.

small, scattered sparks of hope.

no one loves me like You.

for You so loved the world,

from a throne to a cradle

You came and made a home with these broken pieces
of my heart

and You hold my dirty hands.

surrounded by hate,

You are love.

no one will love me like You do.

far too big and far too wide.

you are a product of God's limitless creativity.

perfect thirty-three.

just as you were once little,

He was too.

the boy Jesus discovering the world.

admiring the blades of grass and squinting His eyes in
the sun.

He walked and spoke and grew,

just as you know how to do.

He hugged and touched and felt and healed!

i wonder if He preferred morning or night,

spring or fall?

He had to have thought of these things too,

just as you do.

far too big and far too wide.

may You change eternities

and flip the trajectory of the lives i have come to know.

how can you see the stars

and look upon your future

and feel the sun on your skin

and talk to children of curious minds

and hold the hands of the elderly

and watch the sun set and rise again

and hear the simplicity of laughter

and sing your favorite song aloud

and make a stranger smile

and smell coffee and books and flowers

and stand atop the tallest mountain

and hear the waves crashing

how can you experience the world and claim to doubt the Creator of your life?

you cannot deny that the One who designed the beauty of the world did not also make you too.

both intentionally created and only one is promised eternity.

far too big and far too wide.

there is great relief sewn within the seams of today.

i am made new in the image of God

and i will walk through my days professing His love

for as long as i live.

He desires much for you.

He is pleased with you.

you do not have to earn His approval, my dear,

you already have it.

far too big and far too wide.

your strides may be small

but the significance lies within your courage to leave
the place where darkness claimed victorious

and to pursue the streets of gold.

my top ten.

1.   feel the raindrops upon your face.
2.   open your windows.
3.   speak sweetly.
4.   know that it is never too late.
5.   give grace.
6.   share the good news.
7.   respond slowly.
8.   hug tightly.
9.   let the sun kiss your skin.
10. love others deeply and love yourself gently.

for all of your days.

far too big and far too wide.

praise by praise

we will paint the world,

with His precious word.

may His presence be gentle

but oh so inviting.

nurture my roots

and soften my heart to my circumstance.

show me that You planted me here

to grow into the person

You yearn for me to become.

when i begin to sprout,

take control of my direction.

even when the seasons change,

teach me to bloom toward the sunlight.

towards Your light.

i will flourish in this garden You have made for me.

far too big and far too wide.

although she believed her heart to be far too big

and her capacity for love to be far too wide,

Jesus showed her the fulfilling,

rewarding,

encouraging,

and passionate life

of loving people

and loving them radically.

because in the end

and above all else,

He is the only One our hearts will ever need.

liliana faith whitley

acknowledgements.

i once thought this was a faraway dream. this kind of thing only seemed possible for those with endless time and income. but seeing my pages come to life is a feeling i wish could be expressed with more than the twenty-six letters we know all too well. there were some last-minute additions and some pages that didn't quite make the cut. to me it will always feel incomplete and unfinished but it *is* completely me. it's nerve-racking and vulnerable to share this piece of myself with the world but i will spend my life giving thanks to the ones who made this possible. thank you for seeing my potential and believing in my work. to each and every person that supported my vision and purchased a copy, thank you.

to much of my inspiration. the ones who held my hand when i cried, who laughed out loud and without hesitation, and who wholeheartedly loved all of me. josie kovar, jennifer leza, lindsey duong, micaela kuenstler, senaida mejia, and darla parker; some of you i see daily and others, our conversations are far from in-between, but i know within my heart that we are forever friends, i cannot thank you enough. to maddie parker, who brought me to her youth group where i encountered Jesus for the very first time in my adolescence and began to fully grasp the weight of His love, you changed my life. to everyone at mount hermon who gave me a place to learn how to pray and worship and read His word, thank you. and for your utmost support and undeniable humor; thank you summer staff 2022.

to my family. daddy, mom, david, and nicholas; you are
the courage i have needed my entire life. you give me
strength and hope and humor. we are no perfect family
but who's is? you all are the most accepting, strong, and
faithful people i have ever known. whatever life seems
to throw at us, you've taught me to handle with
patience and poise. there doesn't seem to be anything
that we cannot get through. and to the most present
grandparents to ever exist. some days i selfishly wish
life on earth was infinite, just so i would be able to
know you and hug you for the full length of mine. from
the very bottom of my heart, thank you. i love you.

to the love of my life. kyle thomas holden. i don't have
the words. you have been and will always be the
motivation in everything i do. i love you more with
every breath. your heart is beyond anything i'd ever
thought i deserved and you have a kindness that
reaches everyone you meet. if only the world knew of
your incredible resilience. for your unconditional
support, thank you. i love you endlessly.

far too big and far too wide.

about the author.

liliana faith whitley was born in long beach, california and grew up in the suburbs of austin, texas, blessed to be a coastal cowgirl. not having been raised in the church, liliana found her faith later in life when she reached her teenage years. after giving her life to Christ and through seasons of suffering, liliana cultivated her talents and turned to poetry. what was once hidden within journals and written upon napkins is now in your very hands. liliana's relationship with Christ has become the muse for all of her writing endeavors. she now resides in college station, texas and will graduate summa cum laude from texas a&m university fall of two thousand twenty-three.

and i am convinced that nothing can separate us from
God's love. neither death nor life, neither angels nor
demons, neither our fears for today nor our worries
about tomorrow – not even the powers of hell can
separate us from God's love. no power in the sky
above or in earth below – indeed, nothing in all
creation will ever be able to separate us from the love
of God that is revealed in Christ Jesus our Lord.

romans 8: 38-39